Time Piece

Time Piece

Helga Jermy

ISBN 9781763653016

Cover design – Sophie Jermy, Kitsune Creative Co

Walleah Press
South Launceston
Tasmania, Australia 7249

www.walleahpress.com.au
ralph.wessman@walleahpress.com.au

Walleah Press

Time Piece

Helga Jermy

Contents

I.

To retire: to reach your preservation age,
to exit market, turn rare-river-wild, autumn or fall.

Retreat

So many pages of a life
in the so many hours of policy decisions
and codes of ethics, dissertations,
direct interventions in the quiet corners
of human connection,
now folding into disbelief
chance   revelry   inertia.

I can't remember the weather
or the final words,   locking a door
behind me and going out into the light
with flowers and plants
and parcels of gratitude.
A team waving
waiting their turn in the queue.

No looking back at the magnolia tree
seasonally bare and still dancing,
the sweeping drive
with its red leaves and parking bays,
a sign looming on the rails,
a boot full of children's art.

My aspirations all belong to me now.
Mine.   A curious void.   Time and its
temptations with new primary goals.
To retire: to reach your preservation age,
to exit market, turn rare-river-wild,
autumn or fall.

Chrysanthemums in May

Three days now
between being and nothingness: first month
in a strange void, bad faith or facticity, fly or fall cumbersome,
choice or mired in the entanglement of choice.

       Oh, listen!
       The frogs hail intemperate weather.
       A neighbour's dog howls
       its contestable freedom.

       May the Fourth be with you
       withered in trite but surprisingly agile
       downstream. Laughter as a secret weapon
       chose Ted Talk. Voice as therapy.

The month ahead
in the refutation of time.
Weather is a shower or two with rain tomorrow:
preordained,
blue dot signalled,
erudite as the moon in my stars
which promises an extension of deadlines.

       Default is not my pick. Damn feral
       in the consumption of wren.
       Pink sasanqua buds.

5/6/7th. Minutes click digitally these days,
upright and neon. Time is illusion; relative,
alarmed, quantitate, four-dimensional manifold,
and stuck in a weekend
foggy delight of static sleep-in.

> Across the orb, a man is anointed and crowned:
> a head load of metal, stone, velvet; assemblage
> wild with a sense of the hysterical, heralds
> flagging their instruments.
> This morning's fanfare is a blue flash of wren.
> Stray cat with blood on its mouth,
> quivering its existence with stain.

Eight and late.
All anticipation becomes deliberation.
~~Daytime. Mealtime. High time.~~
The birds here are a community of vagabonds.
Their warnings bear no resemblance to the
philosophy of birds:
though shalt be harmonious
and care for one another:
though shalt not eat your neighbouring species.
A robin is braver than an eagle.

Chopped wood in a barrow.
A flight of towels in the wind,
fraught with the ochre of last century.
In the distance a siren in a singular moment.
Now gone.

I remember that time when.

Bad faith/ mauvaise foi. Floating.

Reclaiming the feminine.

That time when doves cried.

12/13/14th. Thank you for your presence.

Present or eternal. Tense or tenseless.

>   The tram will be here in four minutes.

>   Long, green strips marinated with black beans,

>   the one and only time I eat cactus.

>   Those minutes you can't get back.

>   Six more days of stillness: forecast of cloud,

>   patches of incidental posturing.

>   Faint dragon of cumulus lost in its own fog.

10.30am. Last night's red sky a prelude to a warm day.

All omens are portals to wholesomeness or iniquity.

>   Or so it is written, on papyrus or pulped gum.

>   Driveway drowning in gold leaf:

>   yesterday's transpiration,

>   a maple conserving resources.

Last week a budget here and a blow-out there.

Rare glimpse of platypus by the river.

Invitations on my social thread.

Future imperative.

11.30pm. Your breath on my pillow.

Your hand on my hip.

>   Paws scratching at the window. Cacophony

>   of pine caught in the wind. Distant bass of a band.

>   ~~Bedtime. Bigtime. Timesaver.~~

23/24/25th. Troop manoeuvres, robots in the storeroom,
mauve in the falling cloud.
A schedule abandoned for optical healing.
  My daughter, across the strait, sends an emoji:
   a thread in the dark, a beep in my wakefulness.

The rest of this month is future and tense.
There are forecasts which rely on prophesy, prediction,
prognostication, augury.
Forecast has no past tense.

Camellia will blossom.
There will be bombs and BOM bastardry. The scent of flowers.

Yesterday has slipped into the poetic.
  Today the maple leaves are blush and gold.

A single gull, a flock of gulls

A single gull and me.
Salt air   high tide   a strait whistle of confusion.
Backwards   forwards   shell on polished stone on wood.
Drift and bleach.

Teen boys confess to arson.
An oath keeper and a distant incursion
are beyond my understanding.

A flock of gulls now
darting across waves avoid the news
settle instead on a shoreline declaring indifference.
Crab art maps the sandbars.

Unretirement is not an option
despite its rise in popularity.
Over by the tide sea anemones holding on.

Northbank/ Southbank

The road from the airport is fast and wide,
south heading and strewn with shards.
We're late without dog treats.
Disdained for our blunder.

Today was once tomorrow
and we're still trying to catch up.

My view across the road in
is a constant stream of headlights –
mesmerising mechanoid,
surprisingly soothing. Precarious crane
perched on a high-rise roof
is red and restless.

How a train piccolos
this city's rhythm –   brake hiss
and magpie flute, whirr of helicopter
blades and tram track spark.

Darth Vader with red guitar plays Yesterday
by the bridge by the river.
Beer garden big screen cocktails.
We wait for flat whites as gulls wait for crumbs.

Gold class house white and dips.
A graphic arachnid polyverse
will cartoon my dreams.
Someone, anyone, by the water
please push him in, that guy who plays
amplified panpipes every night after midnight.

There are dead

in the new trench warfare.
No names   just numbers.

Half a world away
from this deafening quiet

there are families who I will never know
weary with want.

Tank time warp
mentioned on a newsreel.

Forest wars   closer to home
mourning the loss of natives.

Roadkill in the gutter.
And my eye is watering its pain

while a waitlist waits.
A muscle in the histories

writes the decaying notes
into all our timelines.

Random acts of poetry

i.

A fourteen tree sonnet, composed over time
in a city park by the Yarra, has self-written
its irregular lines and is as yet untitled. The river's
own rhythms pass us in brown wash with black swans.

As we wander through, my daughter, her puppy and I,
the trees keep us in their sway distracted from concrete
and glass as the mynahs give chase and magpies chorus
their song in notes both love poem and warning.
There is a hum of cars on the bridge and before the rain
scatters the tourists, we stop at some random enjambment,
both of us touching the gum bark in a simultaneous act,
a dog looking on. Monty gives a curious look the way
most creatures have us unfathomed and Sophie reminds me
that we are animals too, making it up on the run.

ii.

There are plants we know by name locked inside

an avenue of apartments overlooking the river,

sunning themselves by the balcony glass, cooled

by intermittent air con. Each tree in central Melbourne

has a postcode and an email and a legion of online fans

each keeping watch to report to the authorities any disease

or acts of destruction. *'You inspire me, Lilli-Pilli'*

from some person in New York. *'Would you consider*

your fingers to be your branches or your roots?'

Urban visual forest, purifying air for a living,

does not write back, at least not in a language we can encrypt.

On a rooftop garden a dwarfed lemon tree, positioned

for mindful reflection, has surrendered its fruit to a bowl.

a meyer tree/ between green fern and thyme/ a gift of yellow

Horror / calm

Nuclear weapons cross a northern border.
News is weeping all over us
with transglobal anxiety, but here the sharp
winter air is still. Dark night still.
Horror. Calm. Horror. Calm.

I might lose myself in a book,
each page a fathomless loss.
I might watch a movie in a reclining seat,
depart into wide screen technicolour,
lose myself with avatars into a whale's mouth
looking for answers.

We help a homeless man drag a shopping
trolley of possessions up a muddy bank,
park it behind a tree. A home of sorts.
Our warm hotel is a shame of sorts.
Reality shapeshifting, sliding through
window cracks straight into our line of vision.

Deep sea implosion creeps in.

Claude Road

From your window
the mountain spreads its table
with mist.

Winter has abandoned
its falling snow,
shoos the clouds sideways.

An almost hidden creek
ghosts silently,
glossy and whispering.

A dog named Paddington
peeps through a fence line.
Distraction is a single brown cow.

Claude Road
is an endless coloured thread
as the mountain spreads its cloth.

The sun sneaks through
throws its carroty red
across the newly planted green.

Winter

Winter.   You cold dripping tap.
Clouds wash by flapping their laundry: sheets
of cumulus; spin cycle of sparrows. Monotone grey.

Winter.   Airbrushed snow fractals falling
as slow drying paint.
Naked tree limbs this far from collapse.

From here I can see you toss a tiny, abandoned nest
in some random ball and racket sport.

My heart ticks somewhere
in its little room layered with bone, flesh, skin.
I should chance a walk to quicken its rhythm.

I should squeeze my chilblains
into fur lined boots, tread your white and gravel
game board which once was road.

How the mountain dominates the outdoor show:
ice topped; breathing through its new coat; steadfast.

Currawongs chant to the solstice.
Trees communing their understorey, lateral roots fusing.
Wood burning in the old Scandi heater.

Winter.   You cut glass figurine.
Chill, familiar, flicker fluster, crystalline brittle stillness.
Sometimes snowballs form themselves.

Sometimes wombats contemplate the ephemeral.

Thin ice, gutter snirt, ice melt. Sun shard in the puddles.

Medicinal gelato

The world has cracked its joints –
sigh and heave
gun and fracture.

We can't do anything about it,
says a friend, except whinge
and worry.

As we debate the new reportage,
over wine and gelato
in a huddle on a catch up,

the world shrinks,
along with our health scares –
heart and breasts, eyes and bones

all passing through
clinical corridors and open doors
into the story of us.

In anticipation of angel wings

Preparing for procedure, clinically awkward
with unexpected bivalves, the morning shifts

predictably towards a surgeon and his knife.
After undressing, I'm told there will be photos

to take home with eerily lit colonic interiors.
I am told I will sleep a while and dream

of aquatic locations. I am told to expect
an influx of belly busting gas swelling

beneath tissue. I am offered Bluetooth.
Suspended in solitude while tubes, cameras

and blades do their thing, there's a strong sense
of drowning. I wake without my angel wings, floating.

Hunger chews me into wakefulness but I can't eat—
the pre-diet acrid taste of purgative swill, that sank

the bland jelly, still inducing nausea. Results are a fearful
exchange of biophysical detail without conclusion.

There will be follow up and weeks to wait
before a bored intern offers absolution.

Walking back to the car, my insides squeaky clean,
I wonder if I remembered to get dressed.

Femtosecond

Eyes obscured from the world's exterior contortions,
head in a brace, cushion beneath my knees,
tubular glass in my left socket connecting me
to femtoseconds of galactic red laser, a kaleidoscope
of orbital nerves spinning like the end of days
to scramble my unruly proteins.

Your eye looks so pretty, says an anaesthetist,
a glitter ball, says a nurse, before a surgeon
sweeps away my sugar crumbs, cuts and reservices
sight in a white frozen moment of bedazzlement.

One line short of 20:20 vision, I step out into the light
where the trees have reassembled their branches
into new dimensional bloom. Even my ray-bans
can't disguise the ecstasy of the scarlet bellied robins.

Loss

Yesterday I heard that I have lost another cousin
and I am beginning to feel careless, though full of care.
Death has no need of my sensibilities. A haunting of two aunts
and three cousins in such short time; heart, heart, brain, heart, liver.
We are all so vulnerable in our temporary packaging. Our tears
become an exercise in severed days, heavy rain, slumped inertia,
a thumping disquiet in the wildness of my abandoned garden.

There is a flower for each of you blossoming in the transient blush
of camellia by the leaf strewn path, spring bulbs popping through too
claiming a regrowth in the storm churned earth. A kitten dazed
by car lights seems to have lost its way in the busyness of the day.
Tomorrow I will get on with things, shake my weary head, stride
bewildered and shop like the living always in need of other things.
I'll post a letter and memories to another cousin, lament in the shadows.

Half a world away from ceremony, I watch the ocean rage against the tide,
whisper a scream into the white waves, collect abandoned shells.

Devotion

i.

After Tom Kelly's poem 'Reincarnation'

I'm not sure I believe in reincarnation either
beyond the recycling of elemental truths. Yet,
still the wind carries the birds and their songs
through the same air you breathed
and that air we shared is around me and in me now.

I imagine you out on the white crest of tide,
and I am too heavy to join you; not light enough to fly,
too living for worms, too rich with nutrients,
too shaky to surf.

ii.

After Patti Smith's 'Devotion'

I am a poet, I said, to no one in particular.
I slipped on my surprise,
surprised by the slide of neural mirroring.

There is that brush of snow in the landscape,
that glistening pond, and before her devotion I am
surprised that she referenced deported Estonians
because Martti Helde's requiem – I feel that too.

iii.

After Andrew Motion's 'Essex Clay'

After my father's funeral I also bit the tip of my tongue,
not deep enough for sutures, but enough
to know what grief is.
I let him go.
What happened next unfolds in memory —
if needed my mother would have sewn
the tip of my tongue back on, stemmed the blood,
even there, headscarved, amongst lilies.
This, I know.

A rarely covered cover is a temulent thing

Blueberry gin.
Rock from the bar band
here from their indefectible practice
across the strait where the mangos grow.
Behind us, the river with outstretched view —
monotone bedazzled dusk lit
hills, houses, cruise boat, canoes.
Bridge across the river. Arced lights.
There are statues in the cemetery
that glow inexorably above decomposition.
Out of sight but out there.
Sail away, sail away, sail away.
All newly composed here or covers.
A rarely covered cover is a carillon song.
Boat by the ramp bobbing on the tide.
Suzy dancing with Kim on the upbeat.
Galactic overhead; a web of synaptic connection,
fluid as unwoven glass, a petit point arras.
Distilled neutral grain meets berries
and other botanicals. The room
is shaking. Aircon buzzing. What did Mick say
about diverse categories of spirit?

Dream phase following anxiety binge

Last night I dreamt that the sky was powder
sheer dust / white as falling snow which perhaps it was
shimmer of dissolving self / textureless and ephemeral
brief and iridescent / meaningful and less.
Images dissolve. As we do.
I woke and you were lying there in your own dream state

reassuring in your warmth / gentle breath and gentle man
and I fall into sleep again / air walk through a door
in a dream to impossible blue stairways
possible hauntings / erasure / talk
to the breeze in my hair
with its after flow / of petals in laneways that I recall

as if we walked through them as lovers
with candles / torch in our hands
in a fever / in a flush of heat
in a moment / in a vision. Invisible
as underground neurons of / mycelium
unsilenced by dancing rain.

Limbic and glorious / dream pool with hot springs
bubble breath / luminous /
an upsweep of your feathered limbs.
Just before dawn breaks
just before the corporeal / muscle memory
insistent on lower altitude / puts soles back on

clover grass then walks you back
to the mainstream / I am aware of my waking
into orange glow / into opportunity / green
light into blank white pages.
Awake now / still feasible and fabulous
muted by other choices / voices

another day light as honey / cravings.
We are a word whispering commune
digitally embraced / enhanced / fragile /
furious / fractured by the lark of it all. Sometimes
words just write themselves
sneaky as love / lust / panting breath and spell.
Dreams are for daring.
Life is a loose door / quizzical / phantom as silk
lyrical / popsicle / a pink lipped and fearless caprice.

II.

In the light we are flowers again
wild as canary bloom, bright with yellow.

We are all river

"When you strike water / you strike your own face"
Vicki Raymond from *The Rope, Franklin River poems*

6.30am: I wake debating with myself
about the eco changes of rivers.
Somnolence of quiet flow at the curve
where I meditate versus
the rush of dam flow
for our power needs.
Here is the captured flow
in my tap for morning coffee,
the shower head's warm therapy.

The Forth flows from the Pelion,
over seven dams, under bridges
of steel
and wood, over limestone,
around my toes, past platypus burrow,
along grass verges,
around trout, over litter
and cattle corpse, by power stations,
into puddles,
into the mouths of small creatures,
past village parks, under fog
and dew, over
round white pebbles,
by barely sealed roads,
through sewerage pipes,
into a wide sandy bay.
Quick, quick, slow,
a pluck on violin strings.

The river is looking confused at the
         U-turn, escaping into clay banks
               or eddying about in circles driving
                        the fish crazy in its dance.
                  Will we drink that stir of crazy
         when it meets our dinner plate as salmon?

We are all river,
         the damp within us,
                  the 60% wetness we drank
                        in bucket loads or stole
                  from the moist sky
                        before it could reach another flow.

I can feel fish scales in my skin,
         toxins in my blood.
                  When I melt, I am water,
         womb, snow milk, sun stream –
                  a steamy down drift, a polished bone.

Fauve in the torn sky

Maddened the sky:
    dawn crimson green
    blistered
at the very top of blackwood trees
 where some majestic vocal flock is
            triumphant?
            jeering?
            plotting?
            flustered?
Unfamiliar with their tone
I'm stunned in the colour
of this brief act of theatre.

Pademelons,
        unruffled by feathers,
        tug at clover root
        as the lorikeets bow out
and venture west,
        their turning road
        in the changing light
            a fauve dashed brush line
                spilling into silent white.

Forth at night

(After Shane Wolfe's Forth at Night drawings)

Spectre-free, but eerily lit
a charcoal breath is
reimagining this lush night –
its pademelon theatre,
its strange sounds of wind in bracken,
its signage bent in the ache of years,
its winding pathways leading home.

Brush stroked night and we're sleeping.
Shane walks and takes photographs
of puddles in rain — of dark
secret places where bandicoots hide —
where the boobook reigns but merges
into bark and wind.

Drawn trees have found us wanting —
the blackwoods and maple, ash
and pine, their tossed boughs in dark,
a pruning in our imperfect vision.
Worn twigs fly like moth wings of grief,
while roots grip the weight of time
in mossy wet clay with rabbit holes.

A smudge of grey on our fence line.
Weedy waves of line. Stones scattered
with tyre-marked abandon. Dry or damp,
the possums spread their rumours and little birds
hide in cupped architectural vines
dreaming of life in eggs.

In the light we are flowers again
wild as canary bloom, bright with yellow,
unfurling the day into petals.

Will the birds tell?

In the sun I am still the snow
cold white of my ancestors.
Ski and skate, fur covered and brine.

There are pine forest paths in my veins,
mapped memory of ice lakes
near the border rivers and runes.

Strange words are sung in frazzled air.
Wind freezing my cheeks.
Brief summers spritzed with cornflowers.

Auroras might steal my sleep
before the long dark nights of winter
tempt me to hunt with fox and lynx.

Here, inversed with wallabies,
my shaky fables are the frost on the trees.
I spin my myths where the new roots hold me.

Will the plover tell the red-throated diver?
Will the goldfinch tell the galah that I've pushed
my boundary to smell the Huon pine?

Sassy birds

I am in a tangle, culling ivy, preserving apples,
flown south from blizzard and black industrial rain
to where sand is an endless shimmer and the birds are sassy.
I find a quiet place to park my contradictions.
                                             In twist of green
with walled shelter, strange creatures have seen my kind before,
keep their distance but grow plump on our daily dose
of peelings.
                    Helicopter leaves of sycamore have flown here too,
with strangle of vines and homely redolence of apples.
Our roots are mismatched.
                              The path amongst blue gum
and willow is tender, knotty, wary, full of shadows but snug
as a Derby girl's squat in a hawthorn hedgerow den.

The burning of fifteen giants

Hollow trees, felled this time by fire not axe,
its seedlings require another 500 years.

The water directed only at
profits for wood chip
and, even then, we can chance
it for a couple of days
rather than dive into
reserves that shore up
votes for stadiums.
Bigfoot, Masters Bennett
and swearing Bob Beast,
the Arve Big Tree and others.
The once perfect Prefect

is now a blackened stump, its seedlings
only require another 500 years.

Sifting the fire razed ashes

Pandani curls
      brittle/ showy/ bloom
  on grass woven mats/ flaunting tongue and fingers
  over the heath's cold bones.

Pandani in snow
      camoufleur/ spiked
with ghost shadows gesturing in blizzard
beneath the chattering crow.

Pandani risen
      over lightning/ flame
  roots moving on/ sifting the fire razed ashes
  in a limb surge/ burrow/ growth/ then burst.

Pandani flirt
      old skirts/ new shoots
  a flaunt of unbridled mockery/ muddy toes where
  green meets earth and the sun is alien heat.

Pandani in a temper
      red eyed centre/ those bronzed curls again
razor sharp/ withered in its thirst/ wind blown
yet smug in its calm wild cool.

Land/scrape

Car wrecks are the grave art
     in the far paddock.
  Land is filled with a throat full of poly this and that.

Exquisite blooms of pigface defy the dune tipped ring pulls

   but where to place the soft waste
    of past shelf life —
    popped silver pill packets
     & 127 defunct DVDs.

At the tip shop your recycled iron chairs
wait for more direct-to-rust metal paint.
  (Container dumped direct to ditch.)

 In the sand, hands in latex powder-free gloves
    toss detritus into plastic bags.
   (Biodegradable ad blurb.)

    There is a nature trail along the beach path
  to lull me into self-care with ceramic drink mug

& shops to test my repentance with sponsored lines
      of soft drink and imports.

Exquisite blooms of flushed clouds look down,
    drop carbonised water on the face of us.
   A gull sees fit to drop its waste on me.

Real as burnt/scape

A tree bone cracks in the branching wind.
    The firies are neon,
    the hay is saffron,
    the hills are distant as memory.

A sound scrapes through
    on a bird's wing
    and out of its cawing mouth.

You ask me for a sense of place —
no map will take you there
or hold your liminal healing.

Draw a line,
cast a fulvous halo to the sun.

    The sky is ginger,
    the moon an altar plate of flame,
    the rivers escaping to ocean.

After the fire —
    mourning the loss
    of moss-blanket forest,
        this tree left standing.

Someday afternoon

The trees are aware
that they must turn their inner
informatics to survival mode.
Mycelium looking on,
is increasingly anxious
and given to cellular aerobics.

The skyscape is fat
with cool syntax, bird scribble
still visible between a lexicon of
troubled branches. Space
is just an endless spillage
of rumour tempting us in.

Looking up from this hill
I see the birch has sent out
a taut little shoot, ready to spring
into green. A wren,
ill balanced on its fragile stem,
speaks a kind of verse rhyme,

considers her options
in a universal mosh pit of singing,
dancing particles. The trees know
their place, form, and feathers.
Dust cloud in the distance,
brings me back to dried earth.

Poco

Walking a cat is a haphazard rhythm. Random. Progressive.
Infrequently regular. We walk for two metres, stop to smell leaves
sharpen our claws, absorb intensity of sunlit corners, think about food
and move on. The day reveals its fractals. Our cat rolling in grit, eating grass,
making sounds like flute purr or battle cry. One step. Two steps. Stop.
Then we're flying through the paddock, tripping in rabbit holes, wind in our fur,
a little pink leash between us.

Today, I pass the spot in the garden where we buried her. I find her warmly
stretching, stirring between each sinew and synapse of my being, her little sock
paws scratching my skin, her tongue seeking out salt, soft fur reminding me
of the distance between first breath and last, of ripe rich play and longing. Pet
love is yoga stretched, flavoured with fish, as fragile as lavender roots above a box.

Storm

There is a storm over the bay, though our mood
shines through the grey clouds, the unpredictable timing
of downpours, marvels at the drama of waves
crashing into stone banks and washing onto the path we walk.

Such a quirky town revelling in its watery mayhem.

Refuse to dive into the mood of the strait: it can catch you,
strand you, tug you into its dynamic energy, leave you listless
and low in the tide. Pull on your raincoat and toss it a smile.

On the wall, drops of rain shatter like glass, or was it hail
we wondered just as the clouds called a halt for a while.
Don't think that you have seen better days. You haven't.
We inhale salt air, watch the scribble of storm tide which
is a love poem. The gulls know its refrain but tug out only fish.

Takayna- Tarkine tailings

First acknowledge that no amount
of increased numbers in the dollar column
can sate the belly of economic consumption.

There are precedents, our federal member cites,
for backing the death on death of wild places,
despite these being the same precedents
that brought us to the brittle edge of change.

Consider this, divided members who only see
the future in electoral years, listen to the masked
owl, the devil, and spotted quoll. Tell them

where to hang their hides when the dam toxins
seep into skin and bark, river, middens,
buttongrass, caves and air, as you disgorge
the mineral earth and cut and scar the land.

Listen to those who have lived the eco-breath
of forests, the custodians and guardians, and those
who park a chair in front of trucks, whose fury

is the long-term fury at your short-term ambition.
Listen to the workers too, to whom you offer crumbs
before offshore profit. Offer them alternate
sustenance, a living in our planetary healing.

Wild ocean, here, washing the once pristine beach,
watches the sun shimmer on our fault lines. One day
as we're flicked off the earth's skin like a dry rash

or irritating sore, the water will prefer to forget us.

How the world spins and spins and redefines itself.

How desperately the orange-bellied parrots ask us

to redefine our wealth. Hurry says our devil of choice.

The oak

After abscission, the oak's
bones stripped bare
in northern winter.

It's been so long since I felt this cold,
saw its figure sketched, graphite,
against grey-wash sky.

Fierce weather
is a trauma
through sparse branches.
All our sensations evoked
by elemental truths.
Wind effortlessly tossing
ice orbs, thundersnow or fiasco of hail.

How we hide
from its crescendo,
cover ourselves in recycled fibres –
plastic, duck down, fleece,
all borrowed, all owed.

See, what a spell is winter —
grass beneath crystal robes.
Bulbs hidden away.
Snowdrops peep though
in white disguise — living light
to lure the winter bee.

Here are the ghosts of leaves.
Slowed transpiration.
The oak's sigh.
Epidermal, thermal.
Weather shield
and protein hoard.

Where the squirrel hides acorns, a bird's nest
is now a discarded rag,
the swallows flown until spring.

If we dare to climb,
remember the fragile limbs
crackle dry in the cold air.
      Better still, know our place
is to be grounded.

A branch snaps, bounces briefly
on this crust we walk on. Small creatures
are heading through its pores.
We are all just heading somewhere,
      around the block or around the globe,
      leaving our messy footprints, or just holding on
   in the storm.

Admire the oak with its sense of place,
each fibre anchored in survival.

Quercus robur: its steadfast girth, its earth gripped roots,
and hollows that have hidden owls, ravens, mice and kings.
You have held me here too.

The topographical torment of trees

"Why do I tell you anything? Because you still listen, because in times like these to have you listen at all, it's necessary to talk about trees."
Adrienne Rich from *What kind of times are these*

Normal
has crawled
into the canopy
where the view expels its carbon.

Deep
in undergrowth,
normal
is retreating,
for what is normal if not
always uprooting itself,
detangling itself
from rumours
or isolated
on the parched hill.

Normal is nesting
like a cuckoo in
restricted bowers.

Normal is normally shy
about its changing limbs.

The forest floor
is a lesson
in deforestation.

It is all about the normalcy
of progress.
The roots
are less solid
in the ground today.

In monochrome fog,
where are the oaks?
Oh, the oaks are gone.

I'm told that the bark
of trees is numinous.

Dryads of the forest
are not just for fables,
a forest normally
holds us like the lost
in times like these–
       leaf litter,
       crash of stringy bark,
       whirling sycamore landings,
       invasion
       and whispers in mist.

Stripped back,
how the bones
reveal their scrapes,
their resin indexed scars.
Normal is now
traversing the bush walk path
towards the swamp,
an axe to the trunk canker,
a war for water.

Planting in stressful situations
requires
great tolerance.

Normal is now viral
and decays
on the inside first.

Where the stare nests

Consider the starling:

its reputation betrayed by a love of orchards

its throaty crack and whistle less tuneful than the wren

its glossy black less startling than its hints of purple

its nest a rubbish clutch of grass and scraps

its rabble-rousing migrant party friends

— so we shun their urban living, but forgive ours.

III.

*Old man of the sky, Jumal, in the runic songs
of my blood. So many things to learn
in this world emerging from an egg.*

Continental drifting

In the off season, you might wander backstreets
of Kyoto taking note of the arty manholes
as a catalogue for your curious mind
or allow yourself the knowledge of that
from some other traveller's media flow.

Standing on a Fukuoka hilltop at night,
an image fixed in my travel weary brain:
the sky black as limousine,
the city lights all blurred Kusama polka dots.
A poem there in a temple carpark.

Clockwise or anticlockwise, the time always changing.
North south, our lop-sided orbit changing the seasons again,
all my solstices dependent on an axis point.

It was not until that first day,
new passport in my hands,
that I grasped that the beaches in Spain
are nothing like the beaches of Lincolnshire.
Crystal clear waves on the shoreline
unrelated to the mighty North Sea
which is another kind of music.

Mediterranean of my bronzed youth
where a bolder sun scorched me into new
layers of light, the light of an English seaside
a more mysterious shade of exposure.

Sail boats and liners cruise the waters
of island gods and beneath them
the sunken vessels of lost migration.

Hecate will protect you at the crossroads and will bring you torches
and a key. More trustworthy, I think, than Hermes who not only is god
of travel but also of thieves.

If ever I swim the Aegean,
I will have pondered the rotation of spin.
On steps to a stone fortress, a stray kitten
weaves between the legs of bucket list tourists.
Things were once more venal.
All human borders open to incursion.

The broken pots and tools of earlier haunters
reveal our fragility in their splinters.
Rock and sea. Thunder, wind and rain.
On dry days, samba into morning.

Who decides the length of a day? Flying east in no time at all.
Rotation again; spin, spin and more spin. I try to write
but my words do not understand the humidity and scent.

I swim instead in a Singaporean pool of fiction blue,
trickle fountain cool, pacified by fans.
I try to write but there is a bus to catch to history's
stone buildings and my words catch in my sweat
and blush. There is a photo of me with an autumn leaf
the size of my head. You point me to the architecture
but I am enamoured by russet crush of a giant leaf
and the scripted path beneath my feet.

In the taxi on the way to airport, we narrowly miss
a woman pushing a pram. The driver laughs,
impressed by his manoeuvre, the woman barely notices.
All is discipline with benefits here.
My words will find their own way home.

I meet a Californian who enjoys living on the edge of the map
and never travels west unless heading home.   Flat earth spinning
its myths on an orb. Tectonic plates still moving along regardless.

I could have had a life here
by Baltic Sea. Naked bathing in the river
could have taught me the necessity of flow,
the invigoration of an icy start,
the need for feet to grip the muddiest of ground,
Nakk, that shape shifting water spirit
embracing the fluid changes of tide.
Old man of the sky, Jumal, in the runic songs
of my blood. So many things to learn
in this world emerging from an egg.

Erewash

Take a canal, any canal.
ride its skivvy edges in recompense
for past drownings.

Cuts from the blackberry haul
remind me of the depth,
the stains, all the curdled stillness,

juice masquerading as blood.
Old men catch fish here
and what are the stains the fish eat?

By the canal gates we dare someone to jump
and she does
then disappoints us with an easy landing.

The gallows pub is stained with ale,
the patrons dead for a century
or sallow as yesterday's night shift.

Tables here are covered in crisps and ash.
There are newts to catch
but what do we do with them,

their lives held tenuous
in the hands of the bored.
There are white swans nesting

in the dark shade of an oak by the bridge.
We leave them to their awe
and fairytales.

I'm filled with a burst of home here
with gratitude, barley wine and courage.
Playing pool here with my brother

our dad beating neighbours
at cards in another bar.
Canals make for easy navigations, barge

straight forward,
no need to lose yourself in the curves.
If a houseboat drips by just toss them a berry.

Fox and hounds

A fox passes through a Derby garden unfamiliar with boundaries
and sneaks under a hedge on her way to the pub
where she is familiar with the recycling of food waste and water
left for pet spaniels. Her eyes are darting like headlights
in a half-moon, rough at the edges with star dust as we all are.

In the bar, where I sit with my sister, the hounds are downing
pints of regret for lost laws that allowed leisure hunting whilst
contemplating the Brexit duck and swallow of fake sparrows.
The path through the church graveyard doesn't mind the footprints
of fox and rabbit, the crunch of feral bone to owl hoot.

We're arm in arm on the way home, whistling a forgotten tune.
They freeze a minute to let our laughter pass then continue
to dance into the night without our interference. Just a fox,
without hounds, and a squirrel or two keeping watch in the trees.

The Flying Horse

(for Sue Wood)

Tell me, what happened to the inner sanctum
of this shopping mall, the long-gone Flying Horse pub
now ghosting the shoe racks with petty theft and
drunken ineptitude. It's not ghoulish indignation
to traditional existential midnight encounters with
skinheads that flipped to B-side, but impossible tie-dyed
gizzards of bureaucratic consumerism that wiped the Quant
lipped, fab yule arse, itchycoo groove and humble pie
riff from the central laneways.

The Boat club by the Trent, where is that now?
Where is the Saturday night, the Small Faces,
the Ultravox, Led Zep, Rocket Man and Rod stringing
out the night by a river in a room full of a dozen or so ravers
unaware that they are dancing to a catalogue of legends
yet to strut their beat boat along the flow of larger waves?
Oh, hot pants us, hippy skirts us, the cider and dry ginger hazed
dolly bird feminists midnight tottering along grassy banks.
So cool, the hip hop, flanging, false-lashed brass of it all.
Lyric me dodgy nights of unstoppable nostalgia, a barley wine
mystic freefall devoid of insta-pic permanence, a pop jangle
anti-war graphic rocking my brain's natural environs
like a sudden memory of a pub that lost its wings and licence.

Talk

To hear her talk
you need to challenge the clay
beneath your feet
where the afterbirth we planted
nourished any number of hybrid vines.

       Pain will get me high and drunk,
         she says. she, we, you,   suturing cuts, wiping blood
         putting forward a safety plan, fair, non-judging,
scared we will cock it up.
                  It's all fine for me
submitting for a refuge, teasing my theories.
spending my pay cheque.

       All women are sitting on a gold mine,
         she says. she, we, you   support her right to choose.
         You, we   remove her kids anyway.
         She tells the court we are all bitches.

At the bar later
a debate rages about
Germaine's right to opinion,
and we are still as split as the castrati,
         wearing our balls on our chests,
         all safely underwired now, debating
         the economics of sex.

We are an honest kind of drunk,
we think. Opinions count, we flaunt them.

And then we went to the Bolshoi, temporarily performing at the Kremlin

On every Moscow street, 1981, there is a swill truck or two looking like open soup tureens from our view in the Sputnik Hotel. There are stout women, so comfortable in their realism and headscarves, sitting on each floor by the lift in the name of full employment.

As we wander the city looking for landmarks, we're followed by a man. He insists that he is taking photographs for a travel brochure but keeps a stealthy distance.

In the evening, after straying down the wrong corridor, with added drama from a storm, we're invited into some military reunion like toy trophies. There is borscht and caviar for generals in the penthouse ballroom. Their medals are shiny as gaudy beads. Vodka is spilling everywhere as we try to leave for quieter bars. But no, they insist. We're passed around as a gift of foreigners, a galaxy of aliens, stiletto heeled western fluff. They practise their English pantomime style with grand gestures and much hilarity.

What were they really saying? My memory is a time shuttered piecemeal swill. Only fit for travel brochures. What did he say, that oversized man in uniform, that Russian summer making fools of us?

From time to time it doesn't happen.

My memory says it did.

You cannot throw a word out of a song.

We will be here for a while.

Perhaps it was something like, *never carry a souvenir bottle opener that can be wrongly construed as a weapon.*

We are searched at the airport.

London parallax

There was an eclipse earlier today. You tell me I am looking dazed, and I'm just saying, yes, sometimes the daylight blinds us.

In London all shadows are sfumato. My face is grime smeared, smoke and grit brushed from sore eyes while St Pauls and Big Ben illuminate their exteriors. Across from a clutter of museum transients there is an old bookshop which holds secrets; a courtyard where ghost horses still run across artist studios and notes of piano and violin rise from attics. Antiquities wait to be purchased. Stout volumes collect in dust and awe. There are rooms full of treasure here and we're drawn in like thieves to a world that still lives in our bones. Outside, is the distorted view; light across landscapes blocked by progress.

Fields of Hampstead are now adrift in their history; cartwheels displaced by a constant drizzle of exhaust. Pigeons hide their push pull muscles in fumes, their feathers grey as gristle. They know what happened. In the backstreets, there are weary faces, chiaroscuro faces, shaped in sketchy charcoal relief against the taut refinement of curved steel and old brick.

We shift away, past anxious chatter in the tourist line at Tussauds. Open top red buses scatter slush. We rush along kerbside puddles to get to the park, avoid emerging underground commuters to join the population of ducks and roses, escape the battle grey, tumble into the inner circle of QM's Garden, past white stucco terraces, back into what we know as light.

A veil of tissue papered breeze

Here we are all gathered in the wedding heat
under floral bouquets under light that rushes
through eyes vivid as lantern orchids.
By a lake where gold swims with fins
in harmonious synchronicity, we are all wondrous
with smiling, petals for confetti, lost in the sincerity
of rings. Amongst the frangipani and lily.
A bride. A groom. A living faith.

Later, we are told to expect a hurricane, to escape
to our taped windowed rooms to rest a while
with our screens. A view from our room
confirms the blurry rage of ocean. The universe
demands drama amongst the serene.

We read, read again, the note on the lift.
The hurricane is cancelled!
On the sand a salute to the statue of a surfer
who is god here. Hula night will draw us back
into sunset. Know that the rhythm is spirit.
A veil of tissue papered breeze. A gecko by the pool
that will turn dragon at any sign of disrespect.
A threat of eruption in the distant mountains promises
fire and lava if we stay too long.

Charles Rennie Mackintosh

(A tribute that wishes it were a tributary)

Art is the flower. Life is the green leaf. (CRM)

Can you hold a life in a portfolio?
I want to think so. I've never been to Glasgow.
I'm a student of wiki and purveyor of books but
even in pixels the cellular shines through.
It wants to dance across a dead screen
throw pigment into an office day
chase the dull air into dusty corners.

Nobody wore a bow like you,
largesse of curved silk and nouvelle gestures,
life's ebb and flow in a black and white print
as generous as a flourish of artist's paint.

Your need for fresh air was more than a remedy
for that childhood limp. Flora
in sweeping Scottish landscapes is hypnotic.
See the wave of mauve in the wind, stems as fine
as ink, watermarks of petal in mist and rain.
The sky pursued its own secrets
found a space for you in that clan of thirteen
and then a group of four
looking out
of industrial arc and sweep into light and growth.

Who am I to steal the flourish of your brush strokes?
Can I dare to pay homage with a wash of words,
water the earth where you planted a line of spurge,
larkspur and architraves?

I've read this so it must be true.
You broke the heart of the boss's daughter,
married Margaret instead, and still kept your t-squares and
blueprints in the office of her dad. Your technical drawings
sketched into the Glasgow streetscape in the way that
trees find carbon in their leafy fingers.

It took so long to leave the smog and grime.
Progress has its price to pay before renaissance blooms.
Expanding rooms filled out the city's tall
new composition
with scratched in chairs and brave new tables.
Willow tearoom, kirks and schools
replaced by designs for a Klimt house
and new life in Walberswick and later continental ports.
Or so I've read.
Was this organic or design? Was this the end of a day job and
art's dream mulching?

You left an inheritance at least,
a shock of doorways and arched brick, translations
of concrete, wood and glass.
You can buy a brooch there now, or a bright fresh poster,
some crystallised memory from a print room in modified fibres.

They thought you were a spy, those southerners,
mistook a flash of colour in a time before war
as red flagged sedition. I like to think that
you enjoyed that notoriety, eased their doubts with sunlight,
left little packets of seeds to grow in grey marshes,
threw pigment and tantrums.

Colour is the trap that catches the bee, an ochre glass of sunlight,
a stylised blush of rose. It breathes
life, lungs full of it, disrupts the disease that
cancered the pulse and swallow of your talent.

The leaves above your grave
are a fading shade of Golder's green, beyond autumnal,
a fine, slowly crushing lace, whiplashed, skeletal.
I sent a friend there to check it out
and so I am informed. History finds its own excuses.

      After the art school fire, with the stars appealing –
      Brad Pitt and Peter Capaldi looking for donations to
      wipe away the soot and ash – you are there again
      in the shadows, inky residue like the stippled grey
      on watercolour flowers, tears in the salt, indigo
      hints where the soft light falls. It will take a team
      of experts, Scottish and Venetian, to restore your
      fine exteriors. In the rubble with melted clocks, time
      wraps around linear symmetry and architectural
      form. The Phoenix Centre promises you a future.
      The students sing your praises in paint and clay.
      The city remains your servant;
                    regrafting, celebrating, mourning.

Somewhere in an archive there are seeds hidden.
Leaves are gilded and entwined in frames, on balustrades.

Death is not a broken stem. A tributary flows on
(with or without my rambling thoughts)
in draughtsman's pen; some kind of hyperbolic ghost in ink and wash.

Breathing in salt

I picture her there, my sister,
on the balcony of her room, knitting,
breathing in salt as the air is 100 sea miles
from shore. Her wool is blue as alien water.

The ship is weighed down now with a virus
that makes the world shudder in the way
your spine dances as a ghost moves by.
But there is peace in the cabin, a little reverie
to the metronome of needle spark, a reason to turn off
the aircon noise and dream in neat stanzas of tropical weather
that float off to slightly shifting horizons. All the time she
is losing her land legs and learning the rhythm of sway.

On an island close by, a weather balloon is set be released.
They will divert through choppy seas to see this.

The salt in our stars

I recall gifting my younger sister lipstick and stockings in some ritualistic welcome to womanhood gesture in her mid-teens. It made me feel good then. It made her feel good too, despite any current dislike of beetle red lip-gloss and the absurd contraption of suspenders. Half a world apart now, she directs discussion with other academics on the future of education policy as I ponder retirement from the paid interventions of social justice. She sends me a WhatsApp from her cruise through the Panama Canal, an exploration of the volcanoes of Guatemala, and there's shared talk in the raillery of the familial. Our brother gifted us objects crafted in wood to store my clothes, to shelve my spices and provide a feeding place for her garden swifts and finches – his skills that have carried him through a lifetime of hands-on creative intelligence. Our brother of the middle ground in a vinelike trilogy, still steering each other through the changing seasons. The uterine home we shared is now an expanded shapeshifting memory palace we hold in our blood, our genes an entanglement that only we three share.

IV.

Sometimes this is what I long for; to be alone,
stripped bare in the dark, in the soul language of lost stars.

Everything is flowers

I am feeling
small today —
humble as
sackcloth.
The universe
has expanded
its light years
thanks
to the Hubble
telescope.

.

.

.

Hawkins'
event horizon
is just a blur
in my mind
which wanders
just left
of the sun
and then back
to the river's
agile swans
protecting
their young
as if they
are galactic.

I step on
a wildflower
responsible
for its weedy end.
I step on a tram
with all
the other
small people.

.

.

.

A lone rock
has found it
necessary
to expand
its quartz into
the fathomless
and weary wet.
A ship looms in
from the south
carrying cargo
and a friend
who thought
the distance
vast enough
to book a berth.

.

.

.

She waves
from the
unmoored deck
like a bird in peril,
her wings shimmy
in feathered light
thrown here by
the burning
magnetism
of a cosmic solar
accident.

.

.

.

Beach ochre
beneath my soles.
I must be patient
as the inky
paperwork
(even changed
to tech)
can stall time.
It flusters
a queue
and what is
time anyway
other than a device
of emperors
and faithfulness.

.

.

.

A once eternal
planet is about to
explode and
someone called it
Betelgeuse,
which is not,
by the way, named
for the juice of
beetles but
for a giant's
shoulder.

.

.

.

She disembarks
with wanton
enthusiasm,
two bags
and words that
flutter in waves.
This is a scene
on a dot
on a sphere
in the dark.

.

.

.

Knowing my love
of ephemera
she brings
me flowers.
Pure peony
rescued by Zeus
to be everlasting.
Pollen in air.
Spheres around
planets.
Everything is flowers.

(Title borrowed from Wyatt Mason's essay
on Baudelaire)

Double/back full-full-full

(Winter Olympics 2018. Something about jumping flipping *on skis)*

The Olympus 12 would have been so proud—
providers of winged caps & quivers & bows (useful)
helmets & spears & tridents (necessary)
lightning strikes & thunder (theatrical)
sceptre & veils & wheat sheafs (handy)
owls (debatable)
poetry (go Apollo with your lyre)

Hera in the ambition   Zeus in the zipped sky
the tumbler aerialists' triple-full-flipped-full-twist
with landing (preferable) have qualified

Me? I am less godly
(despite the camera angles turning snow into
stars
floodlights into comets
flying competitors into various shades of
metal)

Farside

My alter-exo-planet
smaller than Earth
is circling a cool red dwarf.
Just circling circling
in this galaxy of spin
as we search for proof of life.

    Our moon is full and drowning.
    The tide is rising splurge,
    foaming fragrant salted fish.

Gales tonight. First rain in ages.
Is there rain on Gliese 12b
my little alter-exo-planet of excuses.
Wandering unapparelled
outer limits is a tilt in the dermis,
still in need of further analysis,

    slippery as oblivion.
    Accept your scars the stars say—
    this planet or the next little plot.

The 80 moons of Jupiter

I wish I had never read that Jupiter has eighty moons.
They are inside my head now and although most have names,
I can only remember five: Ganymede, Europa,
Lo and Calisto, as they are the ones that can carry a life of sorts.
And Eukelade because it sounds kind of tuneful, like Harpalyke.
(Now there are six).

Juggling eighty moons, along with all the other trivia
in my synapses and byways, wakes me at night when
I meant only to chant them as thought blockers to help me sleep.
Eukelade is retrograde and irregular, a muse, a satellite,
newly discovered, a moon still, amongst all the universal stars.
Sometimes this is what I long for; to be alone,

stripped bare in the dark, in the soul language of lost stars.
Moon struck, sky swimming, wondering
about the atmosphere on alien planets, hoping, that
if I am mindful, I will drift into the liquid core of an imagined
internal ocean, iron rich, on dreamy Ganymede,
or into another cloud shifting moon poem.

Orrery

We cup the moon in our hands, shrink it
to the size of a snow globe, a glitter ball of fake gold.

We shake stars into our imagination.
What little gods we are, toying with the orrery
of dream cool night waiting for the sun

to scatter arms full of dandelion yellow
to tilt us back into light.

Danse macabre

#thedaysleavetheirskinbehind

(after Nerissa Lea after Brack after all)

This is not a song by Ghost, my chills are all my own, born of bone ache and colonic warnings. The need to shiver in the indifference of a square hammer is as real as a swirling metaphor of foreboding cloud. Dance with me, dance with me in the evening dark. The music of shifting time, the great equaliser, tap tapping of midnight recess, full fall of epidemic shroud gone, breathless, light moving into shadow dark, your drum heartbeat percussion, moving into winter's wild stage, one dance step at a time. What a way to weave into unpredictable predictability, holding hands, bones cracking, not knowing when the wind will change or when our colours will mute into monotone silence.

As the dark swings back to morning light, to spring, to fresh air, to one season stepping into another, to a flare of sure footed polyrhythmic, syncopated sight and sound, see the glow of their grief shed skin skulls no longer reflecting mine. Not yet. So warm here in my true impermanent light. Sun drunk on the beach. Lungs full of breath. Skintight and soft. A third age artfully juggling drama. My pearls are back in their box for now, that reliquary of lost gems.

Poet's confession

The real me is a calamitous flapping sparrow
in the dirt water of an outdoor bath. The real me expands
sometimes into eagle claws, scratching and gathering prey.
Claws clutching at concrete, syntax, elisions.
The real me will often press |send| prematurely as words divulge
their vowels and pretensions and an alter me applauds
a poem's confession. (Edit - too many 'ands'/ use ampersands? No.)
I have wandered into pink lakes of certainty unbothered by the chemical
imbalance of coloured water if it presents as art installation.
My neurons hide normality if it interferes with process.
Process hides inside my lack of need for perfect punctuation ::
At times a leech gets in to let the blood flow.

Writing about all our houses, I pour myself a glass of wine
and escape into Netflix waiting for Stranger Things to flip me sideways.
Ah, the demogorgon advises against bricks and mortar, recommends
permeable floors and general disruptions to inter-relational healing.
I need to let in some light. Refraction. Slowed light through a window.
A shed towards understanding. The real me avoids exposure.

How do I escape the 'real me' repetitions without changing direction?
Fuckit. Keep swimming. Let in the barnacles.
(Birds, leeches, barnacles? Edit? Umm...) (And for balance this stanza
needs another eight lines. Doable. Make this line a short one.)
The real me is a gaud like echo in my nautilus chambers.
The real me only confesses through plexiglass screens at the aquarium.
I have photos from the Melbourne aquarium. I must go back there
to confess my admiration for the fluorescent jellyfish and sadness
for the trapped penguins tapping a gig for fish. There is a poem in it.
And the nautilus. Half a billion years of very little evolution
but who needs it when your dreamy tentacles dance in and out of spirals
for three decades perfecting tropical bathing while snacking?

'All our houses' for a themed competition. Do I even like themed comps?
My house is made of skin, bone, flesh, melancholic blood, a thatch
of grey dyed brown. 'Our' feels a bit too much like trespass
but I like to see into your dusty corners. The real me is transparent like a simile.
The real me wanders close to looking for meaning, holding on to fragments
of bird life, or, at a pinch, a flapping sheet. (Edit. Too many commas?) |Send|

Acknowledgements

'In anticipation of angel wings' was shortlisted for the Bridport prize UK 2023.

'Femtosecond' was longlisted for the Liquid Amber poetry prize 2024 and previously published in Liquid Amber's anthology *The Poetry of Change.*

'We are all river' was previously published in *Plumwood Mountain Journal.*

'Where the stare nests' was previously published in *Island Magazine.*

'Talk' was previously published in the *Hunter Anthology of Contemporary Australian Feminist Poetry.*

'Charles Rennie Mackintosh' was previously published in *Rabbit Journal* and *Australian Poetry* anthology.

'Double/back full-full-full was previously published in *Rabbit Journal.*

Some of the poems originate from work in the Tasmanian poets' collaboration, 'The More Than Human Project', curated by Kristen Lang in 2020 in collaboration with *Australian Poetry* and *Island Magazine.*

My sincere and continuing gratitude to the editors, judges and publishers of these journals and anthologies.

I would like to express my thanks to Ralph Wessman, Kim Nielsen-Creeley, Kristen Lang, Anne Collins, Jane Williams, Colin Berry and Cameron Hindrum for their continuing support and opportunity within our Tasmanian community of poets. Thanks to my daughter, Sophie, for her creative flare in providing cover art for this collection and for my website design, and to Pete and Sophie for their warmth and ongoing love.

Helga Jermy bio

Helga Jermy is an English-Estonian poet now living on Lutruwita-Tasmania's northwest coast where rural farmland and wild seascapes contrast greatly with the English industrial towns of her earlier life. Poems have appeared widely in literary journals and anthologies, and her work has been shortlisted/longlisted in major national and international prizes.

Website: helgajermypoetry.com.au.